PETALS OF LOVE

Petals of Love

Delaney Bowers

For my daughter, Ellie.
You are the light in my life, and the person that drives my success.
I am forever thankful for you.

To my teachers who sought out to guide me, thank you.
For educating me, accepting me, and pushing me toward success.

To Mitchell, thank you for inspiring me, believing me, and always being there without fail.
You are a true example of honor.

For my friends who shaped me to be who I am today,
Without you I could not have written these words,

Thank You.

This book is dedicated to every single person who finds guidance, acceptance, and power in themselves after turning the last page.

One Day

I stop and think while brushing your beautiful brown hair,
One day she won't want me to do this anymore.
A time will come where "mommy" will turn
To "mama" then "mom".

Where tiny voices will become big,
And tiny feet running will walk.
I stop and think how she won't always want me to snuggle her,
How she will outgrow wanting to sleep in my bed at night.

When bath time will turn to showers, shaving, and skincare,
How reading before bed,
Will disappear into talking to her friends.
I stop and think how playing in her princess tent will fade away,
How Mickey Mouse will eventually be outgrown.

That car concerts with mom,
Will be replaced with memories with friends,
How my love for her will continue to grow just as she does.
I stop and think of all the moments that will cease to exist,
The ones so tedious in the present that will be deeply missed.

I ponder about the future and pick the hairbrush back up,
So I can cherish brushing her beautiful brown hair once more.
To exist in awe,
Of the beauty of being a mom.

Sunshine

In the bright yellow light of morning's embrace,
Love awakens with a gentle grace.
The sun dances on the freshly mowed grass,
Sharing secrets as the moments pass.

Hearts entangled under the rays of sunshine above,
Together they shine.
Golden light shining in every glance,
Love and sunshine in a timeless dance.

Pretty

She's so pretty.
She has warm, glowing, imperfect skin.
Beautifully thick reddish brown hair.
Rosy cheeks, a bright smile and eyes that resemble marbles.
She has freckles along her body perfectly placed.
Faded stretch marks, random patches of hair, and acne.
But, she is beautiful.
She is me.

Me

I am my absent parents daughter,
I am a direct reflection of their inadequacies, flaws, and traumas.
I can't help but feel that I am too hard to love,
That people will always leave,
Once I am no longer full of smiles and joy.

That somehow I am too much and not enough at the same time,
That I feel scared to believe the words people say,
 For I've been hurt one too many times.
For I always have worry floating around in the back of my mind,
That I can't help but be scared to be vulnerable,
 Over the thought of once again being betrayed.

There is so much love inside me,
Just begging to be shared,
What if the love I am offering is no good?
What if it makes them wish me away?
What if I lose them?

Incredible

It's an incredible thing, loving you.
Watching you grow, change, and transform,
You are a beautifully perfect mess,
I'm glad I get to witness that journey.

He reminds me of the first sip of coffee on a rainy day,
The smell of fresh cookies baked to perfection,
Laundry fresh out of the dryer, still warm and cozy.
The aroma filling the room of your cologne,
He reminds me of home.

Mirror

When you look in the mirror,
I hope you see yourself the way the world sees you.
I hope you understand,
How loving you is like taking a breath of the ice,
cold air on a beautiful winter Sunday.

That no matter your mood,
You are always loved deeply.
How when you smile,
It is as if everything slows down for a moment.
The air feels lighter, my heart warmer,
My love stronger.

When you smile nothing else takes my attention,
It solely belongs to you.
Because when you smile,
You always look at me.

Out of place

In a room full of people, I stand alone,
The piece of a puzzle that doesn't fit.
When others are chatting and laughing,
I sit silent for I have no home in it.

Their words rage through conversation like a river in a storm,
While mine are like water trying to move past a dam.
I wade through water that others walk on top of,
Struggling to find my place.

In this place I search for my meaning,
A space that can be truly mine.
For though I am out of place now,
Soon I'll find my voice, and sing the song of others like me.

Wished for you

I used to beg for a love that is now given to me effortlessly,
A soft love, a love that was built for me.
I used to beg for attention,
For someone to love me the way I wished to be loved,
Now, I am thankful to exist in a world
Where being loved by you is the very thing I wished for.

Ellie's Mom

In the quiet hours of the night, I hear you stirring,
I rise to your cries, and snuggle you close.
You look up at me with eyes full of eternal love,
A bond unbreakable, forever strong.

Whether it be chaos or calm,
A steady, unwavering presence I remain.
Teaching, sacrificing, loving,
One heart that will always beat for the other.

A journey of resilience, the one of a mother,
One of giving so there may be growth, together.
A love so pure, so unique, one full of compassion and joy.
The legacy of being Ellie's mom.

Pray

I pray one day our children share your beautiful smile,
Warm soul, and bright eyes,
Hopefully then, this world wouldn't be so dark.

Adoration

I adore you,
My eyes see all of the most beautiful of things in you,
But my soul is where I fell in love with you.

My soul connected with yours,
Then suddenly when I woke up in the mornings,
You were the first thing on my mind.

To share a love as deep as ours is a gift,
I will always be thankful I get to exist in a world,
Where you picked me, and I picked you.

I may only get a lifetime with you,
but our love will exist for an eternity,
For I love you with all my heart,
But more importantly I love you with all,
Of my mind because my mind is endless.

Symphony

There are quiet moments of the night
where the stars in our hearts align
Our souls in a timeless dance
a love perfectly divine
Your eyes speak what words cannot
And in this moment everything else is forgot
The whispers of our dreams
shared in the hours of dark
A beautiful symphony
our feelings shared a spark
Our hands began to intertwine
a promise shared, a promise kept
In your arms I find my place
for I am infinitely blessed
Through the trials and the calm
we set sail
For when we are together our love will never fail
In your eyes I see a home
With you my dear, my love will never roam

Absent

There's an empty space in every place waiting for you to fill it,
Your absence speaks louder than the words that fill the room.
There's an empty chair at the table,
A void that is always felt.
I think of you when I look at strangers,
I see the stories of all the other fathers.
The fathers who showed up, who wanted to,
The ones who fought hard to stay.
I try to piece together the puzzle of you,
Looking for the pieces of what could have been,
But never was, never will be.

Your absence is a heavy weight,
One that shows no restraint.
Yet in the space full of your absent place, I find strength,
In knowing I can be whole, even without you.

Pressure

    I feel a constant pressure of not being good enough
    Not living up to unreachable expectations
    that others have set for me
    Not being the first choice
    or even the second
    Not being the best at any one thing
    I live my life with an immovable weight on my shoulders
    But time and time again
    he reminds me that I am more than enough
    Reminds me that I am deserving of everything good
    and that he loves me
    For each time he says that, the weight feels lighter

Independence

In the peaceful moments of dawn,
I see myself, raw and plain.
I've removed my mask, there's no act,
Just the spirit of who I am.

I've embraced my flaws, become content with the scars,
For the scars are simply my story etched in my skin.
Each one unique to a chapter of my survival,
A testament of who I am, the book of me.

I look in the mirror and I see strength,
A strength formed within.
I look in the mirror and I believe I am enough, complete.
A soul, a person deserving of love, simply as I am.

Bed Rotting

I lie here in the quiet of my room
Everything so still
I lie with the heaviness of my emotion
Snuggled up with grief and longing
I stare at the blank ceiling
It reflects the emptiness back directly into my chest

Time moves slowly
As if the clock is being rewound over and over
As each minute passes the tears fall harder
Slowly forming a puddle on the
Pillow beside me

I lie imprisoned in my bed, unable to move
Once sanctuary now I find myself confined to it
Holding me tightly in its embrace
My thoughts a jumbled mess, dark, and angry
The storm rolls in and consumes me in my entirety

I fight for a while and ultimately cannot escape
I succumb to the storm inside
I wish for the light, warmth, to be at peace
But remain bound to my bed by the weight of emotion
Begging for release

Gone

Gone like the wind without a sound,
No trace, it's lost, and nowhere around.
My joy is missing just waiting to be found,
I search and search and come up empty handed,
For my joy is gone and I'm left branded.
Depression, anxiety, and anger are all I feel,
I pray my joy returns, all I want to do is heal.
Darkness surrounds me,
I want to be free.

My wish

I hope the next time you take my hand,
You never let it go again.
I hope the next time you,
So carefully choose to give your heart to me,
That I am privileged enough to hold it for a lifetime.

I hope when you speak the three words,
I so desperately want to hear,
That you never cease to speak them again.
I pray when you lay your head down each night,
I'm the last thing on your mind,
And the first when you open those beautiful eyes.

I hope when you search for the light in life,
That I am able to provide it,
That when you seek sanctuary, you find it in my arms.
I hope the day our children are born
You see the incredible gifts our love created,
I hope that when death does choose to take my hand,
It's you holding the other.

Feels

I hope you know I'll always miss you,
I'll miss the part of you that is no longer mine forever.
I'll miss the overwhelming joy I felt,
When people would ask who I was dating,
And I'd have an excuse to talk about you.

I hope you know I'll always be thankful for you,
Thankful for our chapter.
I'm thankful for the memories,
The impenetrable bond we've created,
And for all the knowledge shared.

I'm thankful for existing in the same timeline as your light,
Out of everything, I'm thankful that because of you,
I know more about me.
Turns out I love the beach,
And I have you to thank for helping me realize that.

I've rekindled my love for reading, and baking because you,
Encouraged me to do so.
My heart isn't so hard anymore because you,
Taught me that it didn't need to be.
I laugh a little more,
And open myself up to new opportunities because you,
Showed me that it was okay to do so.

I learned that embarrassment comes and goes
But the memories made last a lifetime.
Why not choose to love the crazy, awkward, nerdy person I am?
Because if you could love her, so can I.

Happier

You make me happier than I ever dreamed I could be
You make life shine brighter each and every day
And if you'd let me
I'd like to spend the rest of my days making your days brighter
Like you have for me
I'd like to show you exactly how you deserve to be loved
I tell you all the time how much you mean to me
But never really give specifics
I'd give my very last breath if it meant
You'd get to breathe one more time
I'd shelter you and protect you from anything no matter the
Circumstance
I'd travel to the high heavens to see you
And go through the depths of hell to heal you
I'd absorb all your pain, negativity and anger
If it meant you'd feel better
 I'd marry you at any given moment if given the opportunity
I'd walk down that aisle knowing in my heart of hearts
That I'd be marrying the very best part of me
I look for the color of your eyes
For things that remind me of you
And if I am ever so lucky
I hope I get to look at the pieces of you
In the beautiful children we create together

If I met you then

If I could meet you then,
I'd tell you that I wish you lived life a little louder.
You don't need to make yourself so small,
To fit into people's unrealistic expectations for you.
That anger isn't the only emotion you're allowed,
To feel and it's okay to be vulnerable.

I'd tell you to let more people see your warmth,
And to smile more often.
I'd remind you that laughter is the best medicine,
That not everything is on your shoulders.
I would tell you to dream bigger and bigger,
To chase those dreams each and every day.

We would talk about worth,
How everyone is worthy of love,
Comfort, respect and happiness.
If I could meet myself back then,
I'd remind her to be kind to herself
And to keep being uniquely me.

My wish

If I could only have one thing in life,
It would be that my children always feel loved.
I would wish them to feel surrounded by laughter,
Warmth, and happiness.

For their belly's to always be full,
Their hearts to be filled with love.
For their conscious to be clear,
And for them to look up to me.

For me to be their safety,
Security, and comfort always.
I'd wish for them to be proud of themselves,
For them to always call my house their home.
I wish to always be a great mom,
A mom deserving of the gift that are my children.

Poet

I'm not much of a poet,
I'm always struggling to find my style, my niche.
I'm constantly looking for the spark I lost somewhere,
Still searching for the love I gave to the boy who didn't want it.
People will tell you I'm distant and cold,
Some people will say I'm too scared to let them in.
I've spewed hate to people who didn't always deserve it,
I've thrown punches for people who wouldn't do that for me.
But I learned how to be more creative in my emotional outlets,
I may not be a great poet, but I'm looking for the poetry in life.
I'm looking for the moments that give me butterflies in my belly,
And the ones that make my heart skip a beat.
I'm looking for the beauty behind people's eyes, how the sunsets remind me of the things I love,
I'm looking for the love I give
To be returned in the most unexpected of ways.
I may not be much of a poet,
But I look for poetry in everything
And there's absolutely something poetic about that.

Growing

I hope you continue to find the beauty in life's hardest moments,
No matter how dark things get, see the light within yourself.
That when love chooses to find its way to you,
You're always in a position to accept it openly.

When problems arise,
I hope you always have the tools needed to overcome them.
I wish for you a very happy life indeed,
A life full of sunshine,
The kind you bring with you wherever you go.
A life with beauty, prosperity, and all the bright places,
One that is worthy of your love, of your light.

Smaller

Sometimes the world takes a good person
And convinces them they are worthless
Sometimes people degrade you so much
That you begin to hate yourself
Sometimes people push and push until
You feel so small that you can't breathe
Sometimes we internalize other people's opinions
So much that we believe them to be our own
Sometimes people don't know how to escape those thoughts
And it pushes them over the edge

So be kind,
Because sometimes people lose that internal battle.

Enough

You are enough.
You were always enough.
You were enough when he looked past you as if you didn't exist.
Enough when your mom told you your brother was the favorite.
Enough when you were never picked first in sports.
You were enough when you were the backup friend,
Who never quite had their place.
When he cheated on you,
 Told you it was because you weren't enough for him, you were.
You were enough when your dad didn't choose you.
You were enough when you looked in the mirror,
And felt empty inside.
You were enough when you compared yourself to others,
And wished to be different.
Enough when your dad showed up for your siblings, not you.
Enough when you didn't make perfect grades.
I know it hurts.
I know you're angry.
I wish I could give you a reason,
Something to make you understand why people are cruel.

What I can give you is this;
Your worth was never determined,
By how someone else views you, it never fluctuates.
It's yours to have.
You were never unworthy, you are always enough.

Chest

I was loved by a man who couldn't love himself yet,
And I carry that with me real deep in my chest.
I put trust in a man who hadn't had that yet,
And it's something that I don't think I could ever regret
I waited for a man who couldn't love me back.
Now every day I sit and wonder if he will ever love me back.
I held a man close protecting him from attack,
Now I'm bruised and battered contemplating taking a step back.

Special

And then one day I realized why your love was so special,
You love me in all the ways that I don't.

Finally

Then one day I found him,
A man whose smile brightens my day,
Who's voice could instantly calm me.

The one who I run to instead of run away from,
Whose arms provided comfort instead of harm.
The man who loves more than he harms,
A man who saw my vulnerability as a strength,
Instead of a weakness.

Who sees my power as beautiful instead of scary,
Whose words are always uplifting and never degrading.
The man who softened my rough edges,
And braves the darkness with me.

The one who holds my heart carefully in his hands,
Protecting it from harm.
I found him,
I may have been loved before, but his love was louder than pain.

Companion

The clock of my life started the moment I met you,
Within your heart, I am lucky enough to find my home.
Lucky enough to find my souls most true companion,
I not only found a beautiful love within you.
I found friendship, compassion, kindness, and identity,
I will forever be rewinding the clocks to the moment I met you.

I want you

In the center of me you'll see a girl that just wants to love you,
You'll see it in the way I look at you.
With how I smile whenever you are near,
How my tension disappears when I pick you out in a crowd.

You'll see it in my inability to stop staring at you,
And in my blushing cheeks when you compliment me.
With every meal I make you,
And every song I sing to you.

You'll see it in the back scratches, admiring glances,
And thoughtful messages.
In the dreams I share, books I recommend,
And "this reminds me of you" texts.

You'll see it in my nonstop talking,
Because I'm so excited to tell you about my day.
In the random facts I share because the nerd in me needs to take,
charge every once in a while,
In the center of everything I do, you'll see that I love you.

Angry

I was once an angry girl,
Angry with my life, with myself, my family.
So mad at everything, everyone, for making me so full of hate,
I was never good enough, no matter how hard I tried.

I never quite fit in with my peers,
Always the least favored sibling in any given situation.
My academic achievements were never thought to be my own,
All my success was taken from me,
And claimed by my mother and father.

I was always second to someone, never coming first,
If it wasn't something my mother wished me to do,
It never held any merit.
I was then placed behind other people in more aspects of my life.

Was never someone's "best" friend,
Was never enough in my previous relationships.
There was always more to be had than I was able to give,
When I wasn't enough it was sought out elsewhere.

In the dark storm,
In that anger I was given you.
I was given someone who chooses me, loves me,
And encourages me.

Someone who is proud of the success that I claim as my own,
Proud of me for simply being me.
Never asking for too much and always giving enough,
Teaching me in a way that was enlightening and not arrogant.

Giving me comfort, safety, and confidence ,
I was given my better half.
My favorite good morning, my laughter and my soul.
I was given the very best blessings a person could ever receive.
I was given you.

Every day is a new adventure,
One I am eternally thankful to share with you.

In love with you

I don't love you just to love you,
I love you because on rainy days,
Your smile is the brightest thing outside.

I love that when you hear a specific song,
Your whole mood changes,
I can see the happiness grow in your eyes.

I love that you make time to appreciate those you care for,
Regardless of the personal sacrifices you may make.
I love that since the day you walked into my life,
You have remained a permanent part of it.

I love the laughter that fills the room,
The competitive spirit and the way
that when you look into my eyes, I feel at home.

Every day I wake up excited for the new day that I get to spend
learning, loving, and growing with you,
For I believe that we were soulmates in another life.
I believe that in our next life I will find you,
And love you with my entire being the same way I do now.
For my love will exist equal to an eternity.

Journey

One day you will be proud of who you have become,
You will be proud of the journey you went on to get here.

Swimming in love

In the quiet moments of my solitary life,
An unexpected moment turned to paradise.
A spark ignited there's was a flame brand new,
In her heart where darkness grew.

Unexpected, and somehow so true,
In your gaze, I found a world so new.
Surprised by your love, that found its way,
Into my heart and I'd like it to stay.

Our love grew fast, but it is so defined,
For our souls seem forever entwined.
There was a rush of feelings, in a short time,
But soon I realized, you were my lifeline.

Time stands still, everything else is a blur,
When you hold me in your arms, I'm superb.
I may have fallen quickly, but those feelings are felt deeply,
For in a single instant, I loved you.

Storm

When the sky is filled with storm clouds,
And everything is dark,
You are my sun.
When I am lost in the darkness,
Feeling hopeless and alone,
You are the light,
And I will always look for the light,
When I am lost in the darkness.

Storm inside

In the hidden shadows of my mind,
There lives a mirror cracked apart.
Its reflections distorted, warped,
A self portrait perfectly painted with detestation.
Each flaw magnified in the reflection,
Every mistake out in the open.

Fears come to life and whispers of doubt circle,
Louder and louder the voices continue
Lost in a maze full of self hatred and criticism,
Where is my worth?
The battle rages on, it feels relentless,
I'm still seeking peace in a storm of self hatred.

Heart

I have a giant heart,
Sometimes I really hate it.
I apologize for things that aren't my fault,
I overthink everything,
Worry about people who don't care about me.
I feel guilty about things I can't control,
Sometimes I feel lonely.
I'm scared I'll never find someone
Who loves me as deeply as I love,
I have a giant heart.

Wrong people

I am not angry that I gave my love to the wrong people,
For they were the ones who needed it the most.

The Least Favorite

In the shadows of my family tree
You will find me
Located in the corner
A place where sunlight is scarce
A place of judgmental stares
Always the least favorite
The one who is overlooked
The one whose love was given elsewhere
When the room is filled with laughter
I stand frozen in a silent manner
My resilience was born
Out of the strength in my solitude
Born out of the anger
Of never being picked by mother and father
Forged in the tears I shed
Each time I was let down and forgotten
For I may never be the chosen one
But I have claimed my place as the
Forgotten one

Rebirth

I used to be a force, or so I thought,
I used to wake up believing I was on a path,
Leading to the brighter future I so desperately crave.
Now I wake up and wonder what I'm doing, where I'm going,

I feel like the weight of the world is on my shoulders and
I'm unable to bear it.
Why does the world feel so heavy, and my strength so low,
Why is everything on me?
When the weight of the world feels too much, what do you do?
Because lately it feels like I'm falling apart and cannot gather the
Pieces together to keep going forward.

Brutal Honesty

Brutal honesty is a knife being stabbed,
Repeatedly into my already broken heart.
Brutal honesty is saying the things that hurt someone else,
Because I need to protect myself.
Vulnerability is something I've always feared,
Something I often find myself incapable of being.
Brutal honesty forces vulnerability,
It forces you to feel the scary things.

Brutal honesty is the way I would tear myself in half,
If it meant I could heal the parts of him that are broken.
It's the way my heart has never quite been whole,
Since the day I lost that part of you.
The way I would give anything in this world to feel whole again.
It's screaming at the top of my lungs to the gods,
Asking them what lesson I am meant to learn from this.
Crying, begging and pleading for answers to questions
 I never wanted to ask.

Brutal honesty is me wishing I could hate you for the way I feel.
Brutal honesty is me praying,
You'll wake up one day, realize we were meant to be all along.

Drowning

I'm drowning,
I'm sinking under the surface fading away out of existence.
I'm screaming for air and begging to breathe,
I'm fighting with everything in me to be okay but I can't breathe.
I can't sleep because when I close my eyes everything goes darker and darker,
I can't eat because my body is fighting so hard just to stay afloat.
Just to live to fight another day,
I'm drowning and the only thing I want to save me is you.

Universe

The universe sends signs in weird ways,
You keep asking yourself
"do I have everything I want, and need right in front of me?"
The universe put us together for a reason,
The reason being to be loved.
To always have a partner in your battles,
One that gives their unwavering support.
To have a constant reminder that you matter,
Of your importance to someone outside of yourself.
The universe reminds you of the things worth cherishing,
The bright ones.
Sends signals from the stars guiding you,
Providing you an eternal home on your path.

Inferior

I've never had a problem being good enough,
At least not in almost everything I do.
To feel inferior to someone who is a stranger is so hard,
Why do I compare myself to her in categories I couldn't possibly compete in?

I set the bar when it comes to so many things,
So why do I feel inferior?
Maybe it's the way she makes him laugh,
Or the similarities they share.
We have ours too, but it doesn't feel the same,
I make him laugh too I tell myself,
But he lights up when she's near.

We have so much in common I tell others,
But somehow that doesn't seem like enough.
She hadn't even heard of me until we spoke,
Maybe I feel inferior because he doesn't tell people about me
Like I do about him?

Maybe I feel inferior
Because I'm constantly trying to make others happy,
While always coming in second place.
Inferiority is hard because I shouldn't feel this way,
I shouldn't stand in the mirror and target my flaws.

He should be allowed to talk to others
Without me feeling unworthy of him,
But it stings so much to know I wasn't enough before,
So what makes me enough now?

Rivers

When he tells you he misses you, that he'll never hurt you again,
Tell him about the River of tears you cried.
Tell him how you asked yourself over and over again,
Why you weren't enough,
Tell him about the sleepless nights of terrors and heartache.

About weight loss, stress reactions, and depression,
About how you couldn't stand to look at yourself in the mirror.
When he tells you he loves you politely tell him that if he did,
You would have never cried the river of tears that he caused.

Falling in love

I hope falling in love is everything you dreamed of and more,
I hope it's like being carried inside,
When you fell asleep in the car,
Waking up in the comfort of your parents arms.
I hope it's like taking a bite out of your favorite childhood dinner
And feeling so warm inside,
I hope it's like hearing the infectious laughter of your friends,
And feeling at peace within yourself.
I hope it's like resting your head on a pillow after a long day,
I hope it's like all the bright things in life.

Poetry

There's poetry all around,
The latte that had a perfect heart.
And the smell of pastries filling the air,
The music flowing through the streets
And the chatter of people all around.
The wind whistling around and
The waves crashing against the beach,
The romance shared between two beautiful people and
Them dancing to their favorite songs.
Poetry isn't something you search for,
It finds you in the most beautiful places,
Life is poetry.
You are poetry.
I am *Poetry*

Inside Me

I have a mother, but never a mom,
I have a father, but not a dad.
I have grandparents that I only disappoint,
And people in my life who wish they weren't.
I have a mother who's sole focus is herself,
Who couldn't be burdened by her children.
A mother who abandoned her duties,
Neglected, abused, and destroyed her kids.
I have a father who forgot I existed,
Who remarried, had other children, and vanished.
A father who plays the victim when confronted,
One who never fulfilled his promises, and always made excuses.
I was born into a loveless life,
A life nearly consumed by the sadness around her.
Born into and grew out of,
Now I grow the love I was never given.

RIP

Rest in peace to the girl I was before I met you,
Welcome to the future of who I am after you.
I clawed my way out of the life that I used to live,
I fought tooth and nail to escape the darkness that consumed me.

I cowered to people my entire life,
Until that anger inside me couldn't be contained any longer.
I exploded my life into pieces, I'm still trying to put together,
Get your glue handy, and start working on your puzzle.

We only get one life, make it yours,
Choose yourself.
The heartbreak you feel will pass,
For the end of us, was the beginning of me.

Child

A child's shoulders were not built,
To carry the weight of a parent's mistakes,
They were not built to be burdened with your trauma.
Not designed to carry the weight,
Of your unattainable expectations.
A child's body wasn't designed,
To take the brunt force of your rage.
Nor their heart designed to take in your anger,
A child's life was not created for you to ruin.

Miss me

And if you ever find yourself thinking of me,
Wanting to reach out,
Typing a message and deleting it over and over
Trying to find the right words.
Don't hesitate,
Don't overthink it,
Don't search for the perfect moment.
Send the message,
Odds are, I'll be thinking of you too.
Wishing to hear from you again,
I'm always thinking of you.

She fell first

She fell for him first
It started with a glance and quick smile
Then a conversation or two
Followed by laughter, smiles and a connection like no other
She fell for him first
She fell for his warm heart, eyes like the ocean, and sincerity
Fell for his constant patience, his laugh, and
His ability to calm her
She fell first, but he fell hard
He noticed her in ways other people couldn't dream of seeing
He saw her light, even though she felt smothered in darkness
And when he kissed her
It was like they were meant for each other all along
It started with a smile and bloomed into a beautiful story

Kind

You are so kind,
The sort of kind that you read about in stories.
You are creative, talented, and so perfectly unique,
I was so scared,
I'd be taking that from you by letting you love me.
But I knew you were the one for me,
When the smallest piece of me felt deserving of you,
Deserving of your energy, your time, and your love.

I'm okay

I'm okay, but I can't escape the negative thoughts.
I'm okay, but I cry when I think of you.
I'm okay, but my life hasn't been as good since you left.
I'm okay, but I'm sick to my stomach from stress.
I'm okay, but I miss you.
I'm okay, but I want you to hold me, tell me it's gonna be okay.
I'm okay, but it's so hard to smile these days.
I'm okay, but I can't stop thinking about you.
I'm okay, but I struggle to look at you.
I'm okay, but my heart seems to break a little more every day.
I'm okay, but my voice is gone from begging for this to change.
I'm not okay, but I could never admit that to you.

Trash

I am trash.
I am the thing you use,
Then toss away once it's served its purpose.
I'm recycled through people's lives,
Never holding a permanent place anywhere.
I'm the napkin you threw away after it dried your tears,
And the empty wine bottle you drank to numb your feelings.
I'm the thing you needed to make yourself feel better,
Even though all it did was hurt me worse in the end.
I am the photos thrown away,
That no longer have a place in your life,
And the keepsakes no longer kept.
I am trash.

Living

For I am not really living,
I am simply alive.

Realization

I realized I loved you
When you were always the last thing on my mind
Before I fell asleep,
And the first when I woke up.
I realized I loved you
When I felt happier in your presence,
And when your voice started to sound
Like my favorite song.
I realized I was completely in love with you
When you kissed me,
And it felt like time stopped for a moment.
I realized you loved me,
When you told me you felt the exact same way.

Begging

I used to beg for a man to love me,
I used to beg for scraps of affection,
The time of day, and everything in between.
Between unnecessary tears shed, voices raised,
And heart broken,
I begged.
These days I fall asleep knowing
I am loved in the way I used to beg for,
And I awaken basked in his light.
I exist in our love,
I exist in us.

Heavy

I would take every ounce of his pain,
Sadness, and stress,
And carry its burden myself
If it meant he would be happy.
I would take the weight off him,
If it meant he could believe he is loved.

Why me?

I lay here with tears rolling down my cheeks,
Asking myself "Why" over and over again.
I sit here and try to imagine a world,
Where our love doesn't exist,
All I can think is how sad that world would be.
How empty it would feel to not hear your laughter,
To see that bright smile of yours.
To feel the butterflies with every " I love you",
If it's a world where you don't pick me,
I have no interest in it.
It's me and you, and you and me.
Always.

Soft

My heart will remain soft,
I will continue to look for the good,
The love, and joy in everything.
For even the darkest souls,
Have a little light in them.

A Dream

You are precisely what I dreamed of,
When I was a little girl,
You are incredibly kind, and chivalrous.
You have a creative mind and soul,
Your energy is that of a firecracker,
Your eyes as beautiful as the ocean.
Everything about you is perfect,
The laughter, sneaky kisses,
The way your eyes lock with mine.
The butterflies I get
When you simply rest your hand on my thigh,
And the sparks that fly when we kiss,
It is simply a dream.

Inconvenience

An inconvenience,
That's what I feel like I am to most people
A bother,
A nuisance.
I can tell when I've overstayed my welcome,
I can tell that my presence is too much for people.
When all I want is to be near,
All you want is for me to disappear.
I try to convince myself that it's not true,
To believe you when you say everything is fine.
Until you open up
And tell me how you feel suffocated and burnt out,
It's an endless cycle I repeat, it's the life of always being an inconvenience.

Parents

I have several parents
Though none of which are my mother or father
A parents is defined as
 "the material or source from which something is derived."
There are so many things about me
That can be accredited to my parents
My personality that was influenced by the people I grew up with
To my habits I've picked up along the way
My drive was given to me from my brother
Whom I always wanted to win against
And my wit from my teachers
Who spent their lives educating
My spite derived straight from my sister
Who was my ultimate childhood enemy
My sense of humor from the friends I have made along the way
My ability to love though, that was all you

Grieving you

The roots of grief burrow deep inside me.
How can I grieve the life of a person who never died?
How can I feel so much emptiness inside me,
From the loss of his love?
Knowing your heart is beating strong,
While mine feels like it's been split in two is torture.
Realizing I'd never feel your touch on my skin,
In such a loving manner again,
Or feel your lips pressed up against mine,
The irony of how never hearing your voice,
Say " I love you " again,
Makes me wish for mine to be lost forever.
How can I feel so empty when you seem so full?
How can I grieve the part of you I lost,
While you seem to be celebrating,
The new beginnings?

Abused

In the quiet of the night I am unable to sleep,
Memories of words that cut so deep.
My childhood was lost to fear,
The pain inflicted on me year after year.

Behind closed doors, their anger roared,
A love that I wished would have, but couldn't soar.
Unseen bruises, tears falling too frequently, living life like an emotionless machine,
My life always entangled in a painfully cruel routine.

A strength within that still exists,
So in the darkness I still persist.
For one day I'll escape the chains that bind,
And leave my abusive past behind.

Spinning

The world stopped spinning when he died,
He died and nothing ever felt right again.
My days were filled with bitterness and grief,
My heart cold, and my mind a mess.
My world started spinning again when I met you,
You brought light back into the darkness of my heart.
You filled the room with so much sunshine
That the darkness could no longer hide from it,
My days started to fill with happiness and joy,
My heart thawed,
My mind began to focus.
Focus on love.

Galaxies of love

You are the sun, moon,
And all of the brightest stars,
When that darkness feels like it's crushing you,
 Remember that your
Light shines as bright as the sun, moon,
And the brightest of stars.
When the darkness feels heavy, think of the sun,
Channel the energy within and push the darkness out.

You are love

In my eyes you are the definition of love,
You are that first sip of coffee on a peaceful Sunday morning.
The ocean waves crashing softly on the beach,
The warmth of a shower on a cold day.
The smell of flowers blooming in the spring,
And the gentle kiss of a loving partner.
You are the once in a lifetime love, my person.
You are the only love that ever made sense to me.

A Woman

I am told I am a woman
I am expected to sit down and listen while the men speak
And do so happily, a smile on my perfectly put together face
I am told to cater to their needs, desires, and interests
Because I am a woman,
I am forced to live in the shadow of a man
Because I am a woman
 I have to work twice as hard
And fight even harder
For the things that are simply handed to men
My body is never seen as my own
Simply a tool to be used
For men to bear their children
I fight for equal pay, equal rights, and the same freedoms
That men are given simply for being men
Why am I forced to hide my thoughts
To appease a man who would never do the same
Why should I fight so hard for equality
In a system designed to stand against me

It's Okay

I tell you it's okay,
I say not to worry and that I'm just fine.
I tell you that it is okay
In an attempt to convince myself that it is,
I wear a mask that looks like happiness,
But underneath is pain.
Underneath that mask
Is a girl who is desperately trying to understand,
A girl who is fighting
With every ounce of strength she has left.
I tell you it's okay
Because the pain under the surface is one I never
Want you to experience,
I'll be the strong one, I'll carry the burden to protect you.

Heartbroken in the Rain

Looking above at the gray, crying sky,
The tears inside the heart begin to weep.
The raindrops fall alongside the shattered dreams,
The echoes of lost love, and those unheard screams.
Each raindrop tells a story full of pain,
Once full of love, bright and gleaming,
Now slowly washed away by rain.
Within the storms cold, and relentless art,
Sits all the echoes of broken hearts.

Burn

That fire you feel spreading outward from your core,
The one that feels like untapped destruction,
 Waiting to be unleashed.
The fire that gets stronger and stronger
With every harsh comment,
Endured and tear shed,
Use it.

Take all the rage, pain, and heartache,
And use it to your advantage.
Mold it into your power,
And wield it like the weapon it is.
Show people exactly who you are,
And how you want to be seen.
Don't let it corrupt and destroy you,
Let it free you.

To be loved by you

To go from being loved by you
To being just another person was heart shattering
It was devastation, depression, and pain
I felt like I'd been thrown away into the garbage
With the other trash you've discarded

It was so incredibly hard because
You took the time to show me
What it is truly like to be loved
Then took it all away

You loved me so well that you are the reason for my pain
Also the reason I can stand back up and live to fight another day
You showed me that I was worthy of someone's love
Even though our chapter has ended
Those memories of us are mine to keep
They are mine to hold, cherish, and love
They are my reminder that I am worthy of a love like yours

Cherished

I hope you know that you are a devastating loss,
A loss that is felt deeply, and often.
Loving you was like turning on the light,
In a city overcome with darkness.

To think of a world dimmed by losing you,
Is one I never want to live in.
You wonder why you,
I wish I could explain.

How I have yet to see a fragment of your shattered image,
That isn't worth being *cherished*.
A piece of you that I couldn't help but love,
How since the moment I met you, this world has been lighter.

It's a devastating loss to be apart from you,
One that I wish I never had to experience.
I never thought I would see a day where you weren't with me,
A day where your light wouldn't be shining in my skies.

Hold me

You close your eyes and imagine for a moment
That he is lying beside you in bed
His soft skin brushing up against yours
Giving you that feeling of
Security you desperately crave
The tiniest of snores, rain hitting the windows,
And thunder rumbling in the skies
Your waist gently wrapped in his arms
Your breathing slows matching his
The softest of whispers in your ear
.... I love you.

He pulls you in closer, tighter, cozier.
You inhale all the love and
Positivity in the room, exhaling the bad
And at that moment, you are home

Strength

It's a hard thing, you know?
Getting up each day,
When you feel like you're fighting just to breathe.

It takes an incredible strength
To get knocked down by life,
And choose to keep pushing.

Celebrate your strength today, you deserve it

Memory

My greatest memory of loving you,
Will always be the way you held me,
When I felt as if everything around me was crumbling.
It is the way you never fail to show up for me,
Believe in me, and protect me.
When I am feeling my most vulnerable,
You look past it and remind me that I am strong, capable,
And that I will be okay.
My greatest memory of us
Is how you loved me despite the struggles,
Bad days, and arguments.
You simply loved me.

Brave

How brave you must be,
To make an effort each and every day.
To never blame your suffering,
As a reason to harm another.

How brave your heart is,
To always be warm.
To feel the fire within start to suffocate,
And be willing to light another again.

Empowered

You are worthy of more than you realize,
And are stronger than you were yesterday.
Your capabilities are unmatched,
And you will achieve incredible things,
No matter than adversity you face.
Every challenge is an opportunity,
And puts your resilience to the test.
Keep believing in your extraordinary abilities.
Place trust in yourself,
Understand you have the power to create,
A positive impact on the world around you.

I hope

I hope one day you find a love that is true
A love that feels like the way a contagious laugh sounds
One full of understanding, compassion and adventure
I hope you stumble across a love unique to you
The kind of love you watch in movies,
And read in your favorite fairy tale stories
One that feels like fresh baked cookies with a glass of cold milk
Or waking up on a beautiful snowy morning
With hot chocolate in hand
I hope you marry the one who's eyes look like the future
And has a soul that belongs to you
The one who laughs at all your jokes,
Especially the ones nobody else understands
Who dances with you when there's no music playing
And who remembers that your favorite color is purple.
I hope one day you feel the kind of love you have always craved
The kind where their touch is an instant calm,
And their voice grounds you.
Because out of everyone I know,
The person who deserves that most,
Has always been you.

Apart

When our love is fading, and our lives must part,
There's an immovable weight, lying on my heart.
Memories of you linger, happy and bright,
It would appear it's time to say goodnight.

Our paths connected, we walked side by side,
Now split in two, we divide.
With heavy hearts, and a soft goodbye,
I watched our love slowly die.

In time the heart begins to know, that letting go is not the end,
Just a true chance for broken souls to mend.
So I say farewell, with love so true,
I'll forever cherish the moments I shared with you.

Vulnerable

I stare at your smile and feel at peace,
Your light shines so bright ,
It nearly penetrates the shadows where my feelings live.
I make a comment that never needed to be made
And your light dims just enough to keep me protected.

Protected from the idea of being vulnerable.
Protected from the possibility of being hurt.
Protected from falling in love again.

I stare into your perfectly blue eyes,
and feel the power they hold over me.
Feel the urge to open up and let you in.
Feel like it's okay to be real, be open.

So I look away and and go silent.
I avoid the future conversations of my traumatic past,
How could you ever see the real me and love her?

I shield myself from your sincerity.
I shield myself from your touch.
I shield myself from your warmth.

I ponder on how to remedy something I broke
Because of fear of being hurt.
I bake you cookies for your birthday,
Deliver them with hopes of seeing that smile,
And staring into the eyes that make me feel seen.
I slip up and start back at the beginning.

How do I tell him that I want to try again

When I've failed to give him a reason to believe in me?
How do I show him I'm capable of being real,
Of letting him know me?
How do I break the cycle of being shielded?

I could tell him that I've dreamt of my desire,
How one was of him
I could say I'm just a girl who needs a little more time.
I could say I just need him to hold me long enough,
That the walls melt away in his warmth,
The shadows are brightened instead of dimmed by his light.

But ultimately, I stay silent.
In silence, there's no chance of me saying the wrong thing.

Nonexistent

I once loved a man who couldn't love me back,
His efforts, misguided, and his mind a mess.
His words like knives stabbing into my heart,
My love spilled out of the wounds he carved into my chest.

I once loved a man who I thought was the best,
He was like everything I had always dreamt.
His life however, was a juggling act,
He juggled and juggled
But could never balance me with the rest.

I once loved a man who didn't know who he was,
He searched for his place and came up empty handed.
He smiled through the pain
And woke up each day more saddened,
For the girl who loved him was being damaged.

I once loved a man who pushed me away,
He needed to be alone to find his way.
The shove to the ground was a paralyzing feeling,
One full of misery and tears forever falling.

Speak

I break the silence, my words pour out like rain,
With each drop falling there's a whisper of my pain.
I speak with a voice that's always lost in translation,
Unheard, forgotten, all that's left is internal aggravation.

A silent scream, like a voice in chains
I cry, I plead, and go unseen.
I speak again and my words are forgotten,
Why break the silence if my words never blossom.

Immeasurable

It's an immeasurable existence of love
I know we are meant to be together
For the sole fact that I cannot stop thinking of you
A constant thought floating around my head
I know I left here to grow and be happy
I never suspected that with such growth
Would come such torture

As luck would have it

As luck would have it, I met you
From hearing your voice for the first time
And how it gave me butterflies
The first time I got to kiss you warm lips
How your touch made me melt into you
And how I feel so safe in your arms
I knew you were so uniquely special from
The moment your hand touched my knee
As you sang to me your favorite songs
How simply looking at your smile made me blush
The way your eyes met mine
And all I wanted was for them to never look away
As luck would have it, I met you
I met the person that made me feel seen
The one who I could spend all day
Talking to and never get bored
Someone who's snuggles felt like a magical healing power
And whose laugh was by definition perfect
They say love is like a dream and I believe that to be true
Everyday since I met you,
I dream of what it would be like to love you.

Finite

    Love is not finite,
    It is ever changing, growing, and
    By definition, infinite.

    I am truly lucky to have the honor,
    Of standing by your side, and
    Soaking up a mere drop of your light.

    You are the good things the world offers,
    For if my only honor of life,
    Was loving you,
    I would be forever fulfilled.

Gift

To share a love as deep as this,
is truly a gift.
I will always feel true gratitude,
for existing on this time line with you.
My love for you is inequitable,
I know even in your death,
My heart would still beat for you.

Joy

Joy is like the sun, warm and full of light,
It sprinkles hearts with pure delight.
A baby laughing, a couple kissing,
Moments filled with endless bliss.

Petals Of Love

In the garden where things that blossom bloom,
The petals of love dance, dispelling gloom.
Each one whispers a tune,
Only heard by me and you.

Softly they fall, like gentle rain,
Easing everything, including my pain.
With every touch, and each embrace,
In this garden, we made our place.

Through seasonal change, these flowers endure,
A symbol of our love, one so pure.
These petals of love are always bright,
They guide us through both day and night.